Pebble® Plus
Bilingüe/Bilingual

TODO ACERCA DEL OTOÑO/ALL ABOUT FALL

# Las personas en otoño/ People in Fall

por/by Martha E. H. Rustad

Traducción/Translation: Dr. Martín Luis Guzmán Ferrer
Editor consultor/Consulting Editor: Dra. Gail Saunders-Smith

Capstone press®

Mankato, Minnesota

Pebble Plus is published by Capstone Press,
151 Good Counsel Drive, P.O. Box 669, Mankato, Minnesota 56002.
www.capstonepress.com

1 2 3 4 5 6 14 13 12 11 10 09

*Library of Congress Cataloging-in-Publication Data*
Rustad, Martha E. H. (Martha Elizabeth Hillman), 1975–
    [People in fall. Spanish & English]
    Las personas en otoño = People in fall / por/by Martha E. H. Rustad.
    p. cm. — (Todo acerca del otoño = All about fall) (Pebble plus)
    Summary: "Simple text and photographs present people in fall — in both English and Spanish" —
Provided by publisher.
    ISBN-13: 978-1-4296-3261-4 (hardcover)
    ISBN-10: 1-4296-3261-5 (hardcover)
    1. Autumn — Juvenile literature. I. Title. II. Title: People in fall.
QB637.7.R8718 2009
508.2 — dc22                                                                 2008034507

**Editorial Credits**
Sarah L. Schuette, editor; Katy Kudela, bilingual editor; Adalín Torres-Zayas, Spanish copy editor;
    Veronica Bianchini, designer

**Photo Credits**
Capstone Press/Karon Dubke, all

## Note to Parents and Teachers

The Todo acerca del otoño/All about Fall set supports national science standards related
to changes during the seasons. This book describes and illustrates the people in fall in
both English and Spanish. The images support early readers in understanding the text.
The repetition of words and phrases helps early readers learn new words. This book
also introduces early readers to subject-specific vocabulary words, which are defined
in the Glossary section. Early readers may need assistance to read some words and to
use the Table of Contents, Glossary, Internet Sites, and Index sections of the book.

# Table of Contents

# Tabla de contenidos

# Fall Is Here

It's fall.

The days are shorter.

The weather is colder.

# Llegó el otoño

Es otoño.

Los días son más cortos.

El tiempo es más frío.

## What We Do

We wear sweaters and jackets to play outside.

## Lo que hacemos

Nos ponemos nuestros suéteres y abrigos para jugar afuera.

6

School starts in fall.

We walk to school.

El colegio empieza en otoño.

Nos vamos caminando

a la escuela.

8

We wear costumes
on Halloween.
We go trick-or-treating.

Nos ponemos disfraces
en *Halloween*. Salimos a
pedir regalitos o, si no,
a hacer bromas.

We celebrate Thanksgiving.
We eat turkey, potatoes,
and corn.

Celebramos el Día de
Acción de Gracias.
Comemos pavo, papas
y maíz.

# Getting Ready

We get ready for winter.

We harvest vegetables

from our garden.

# Los preparativos

Nos preparamos para

el invierno. Cosechamos

las verduras de nuestro jardín.

14

We pick ripe apples
from trees in our yard.

Recogemos las manzanas
maduras de nuestro patio.

We rake the fallen
leaves into piles.

Usamos el rastrillo para
recoger las hojas y
ponerlas en montoncitos.

18

## Other Signs of Fall

In fall, people are busy getting ready for winter. What are other signs that it's fall?

## Otras señales del otoño

En otoño las personas están ocupadas preparándose para el invierno. ¿Qué otras señales hay que es otoño?

# Glossary

**costume** — clothes worn by people dressing up

**garden** — an area of dirt where flowers and vegetables are planted

**Halloween** — a holiday celebrated on October 31; people dress in costumes and go trick-or-treating on Halloween.

**harvest** — to gather crops that are ripe

**ripe** — ready to be harvested, picked, or eaten

# Glosario

**cosechar** — recoger los cultivos que están maduros

**los disfraces** — ropa que se usa en algunas fiestas

*Halloween* — fiesta que se celebra el 31 de octubre; las personas se disfrazan para salir a pedir regalos o, si no, responder con una broma.

**el jardín** — superficie de tierra donde se siembran flores y verduras

**maduro** — listo para cosecharse, recolectarse o comerse

# Internet Sites

FactHound offers a safe, fun way to find educator-approved Internet sites related to this book.

Here's what you do:

1. Visit *www.facthound.com*
2. Choose your grade level.
3. Begin your search.

This book's ID number is 9781429632614.

FactHound will fetch the best sites for you!

# Index

# Sitios de Internet

FactHound te brinda una forma segura y divertida de encontrar sitios de Internet relacionados con este libro y aprobados por docentes.

Lo haces así:

1. Visita *www.facthound.com*
2. Selecciona tu grado escolar.
3. Comienza tu búsqueda.

El número de identificación de este libro es 9781429632614.

¡FactHound buscará los mejores sitios para ti!

# Índice